YOU ARE THAT Tree

THE GARDEN OF EDEN

T.S. CHERRY

YOU ARE THAT TrEe!

Children's Bible Study and Sunday School Lessons

By

T. S. CHERRY

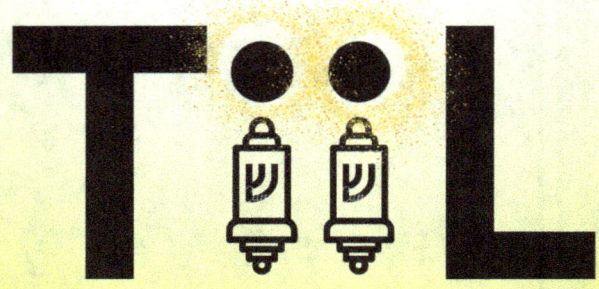

Copyright © 2019 | www.Tiil.org All rights reserved.

YOU ARE THAT TREE!   T. S. CHERRY

LESSON 1
TOPIC: GOD MADE ME FOR HIS GLORY

TEXT: Daniel 4:10-12

MEMORY VERSE: *"Your Majesty, you are the tree, tall and strong." Daniel 4:22a, GNT*

CENTRAL THOUGHT: *You were made to fulfill a specific purpose that brings glory to God.*

Study Headings:

- *Back to Genesis*
- *Made for a Purpose*
- *How Do You Bring God Glory?*

Study Introduction:

King Nebuchadnezzar had a very disturbing dream. It was about a tree he saw in the middle of the earth. He didn't know the interpretation of his dream, and no one else did. That made matters worse. But Daniel was introduced to the king as having a special ability from God to interpret the king's dream.

King Nebuchadnezzar began to tell Daniel his dream. **Read Daniel 4:10-12**

The king said, ""While I was asleep, I had a vision of *a huge tree in the middle of the earth. It grew bigger and bigger until it reached the sky and could be seen by everyone in the world. Its leaves were beautiful, and it was loaded down with fruit* — enough for the whole world to eat. Wild animals rested in its shade, birds built nests in its branches, and every kind of living being ate its fruit." GNT

Five things stand out about the tree the king saw in his dream. Can you mention them?

1. It was a huge tree in the middle of the earth;
2. It grew bigger and bigger until it reached the sky and could be seen by everyone in the world.
3. It had fresh green leaves and was loaded with fruits for all to eat.
4. Its leaves were beautiful, and it was loaded down with fruit — enough for the whole world to eat.
5. Wild animals rested in its shade, birds built nests in its branches, and every kind of living being ate its fruit.

The description of this tree shows that it represented something else and not just an ordinary tree. That is why the king was seeking interpretation to his dream.

What was Daniel's interpretation of the king's dream? **Read Daniel 4:22**

YOU ARE THAT TREE!

T. S. CHERRY

Daniel said, *"Your Majesty, you are the tree, tall and strong."* **Daniel 4:22**

So, Daniel was telling the king that he (the king) was that tree he saw in his dream. From Daniel's interpretation, it is clear that the tree in the king's dream represents a person. All the qualities of the tree are the possibilities in a person's life.

In this study, you will see that what Daniel told King Nebuchadnezzar is now applicable to you. God is saying that You are that Tree!

BACK TO GENESIS

What Bible story does the dream of King Nebuchadnezzar remind us? Can you remember any?

It reminds us of our first parents – Adam and Eve – and the Garden that God planted for them. **Read Genesis 2:8-9**

The Bible tells us that "the Lord God planted a garden in Eden, in the East, and there he put the man he had formed. He made all kinds of beautiful trees grow there and produce good fruit. *In the middle of the garden stood the tree that gives life and the tree that gives knowledge of what is good and what is bad."* Genesis 2:8-9, GNT

YOU ARE THAT TREE!

T. S. CHERRY

In King Nebuchadnezzar's dream, he saw a tree in the center of the earth. Back in Genesis, we also see that God created some special trees in the center of the Garden of Eden.

So, Daniel's interpretation to King Nebuchadnezzar's dream sounded closely related to the trees in the center of the Garden of Eden. And just like Nebuchadnezzar's dream, the Book of Genesis actually begins much like a dream.

So, it seems that, perhaps Nebuchadnezzar was asking for the meaning of what occurred back in Genesis: What is the meaning behind the tree of life? And what is the purpose of the other tree in the midst of the Garden - the tree of the knowledge of good and evil? What does this mean to our lives?

MADE FOR A PURPOSE

Have you noticed that God created each of the trees in the middle of the Garden for a specific purpose? **Read Genesis 2:9** and find out their purposes.

The Bible says, *"He made all kinds of beautiful trees grow there and produce good fruit. In the middle of the garden stood the tree that gives life and the tree that gives knowledge of what is good and what is bad"* (Genesis 2:9, GNT).

1. God made all kinds of beautiful trees to produce "good fruit." So, the first purpose for the trees was to bear good fruit.
2. He made "the tree of life." So, the purpose of this tree was to bring or give life.
3. He made "the tree of knowledge of what is good and what is bad." So, the purpose of this tree was to give knowledge of good and bad.

When you look at the fact that God made the trees in the Garden with a specific purpose in mind, you will better understand the tree in Daniel's vision as being stationed specifically for the manifestation of God's glory.

And if the Bible is telling us that **YOU ARE THAT TREE**, it means you were created specially by God to fulfill the purpose of bringing glory to Him through your life.

YOU ARE THAT TREE!

T. S. CHERRY

HOW DO YOU BRING GOD GLORY?

You can bring God glory through your life by fulfilling the purpose of the "tree" in the midst of the earth, as seen in the king's dream.

Can you mention the five things that stand out about the tree the king saw in his dream?

Read Daniel 4:10-12 again.

I want you to remember that God is saying, "You are that tree in the midst of the garden." So, every description of that tree meant something about your life:

The Bible describes this tree as "a huge tree in the middle of the earth;" What that means is that God wants you to grow into an adult that occupies a central position in the family, business, and in fact, everything. God wants your life to fill everywhere with godly influence, just as that tree was huge in the middle of the earth.

Read about God's plan for you to be ABOVE ONLY in Deuteronomy 28:13.

Notice that the Bible says the tree, "grew tall and strong, reaching high into the heavens for all the world to see." See that? "For all the world to see!"

That's the description of your life, the real way God wants your life to be. He wants you to be in such a blessed position that 'all the world' – everyone around you and beyond can see what He's doing in and with your life.

God doesn't want you to be a timid child. He doesn't want you to struggle with low self-esteem. He wants you to make your life a testimony that the whole world can see and read about. Read Isaiah 60:15

The Bible tells us that this tree had 'fresh leaves and was loaded with fruits.' It was different from one tree in the New Testament that had fresh leaves all over it but no fruits. Read Mark 11:13-14.

Copyright © 2019 | www.Tiil.org All rights reserved.

YOU ARE THAT TREE!

T. S. CHERRY

When Jesus came along, the Bible says, "He noticed a fig tree in full leaf a little way off, so he went over to see if he could find any figs. But there were only leaves... Then Jesus said to the tree, "May no one ever eat your fruit again!""

That tree ended up being cursed. And it died off.

That's not the picture of life that God has for YOU. He wants you to live in a way that brings blessings to others.

Is your life bringing blessings to other people around you?

God doesn't want you to just look like you carry His blessings; He wants you to actually have His blessings and let others who come around you experience it. He wants you as a child to grow to become a person whose life is providing shade to both friends and foes.

Read Genesis 12:2 and see what God said to Abraham about this. He didn't just want Abraham to be blessed. He wanted him to be a blessing to others, too. That's what God also wants for your life. He wants you to be in that place where the whole world is feeding from 'your tree.'

So, when you look at that tree in the midst of the field, you see a picture of yourself. You see a picture of where God wants you to be. You see a picture of the kind of person God wants you to grow into.

CONCLUSION

You may be a little child today, but God did not make you for the low places of the earth. You were made for the topmost height. And God wants you to grow up and be at that height where you are a blessing to countless people. That is the way your life will bring Him glory.

REMEMBER THIS:

God made you for His Glory!

YOU ARE THAT TREE!

T. S. CHERRY

LESSON 2

TOPIC: SEE FROM GOD'S VIEWPOINT

TEXT: Mark 8:22-26

MEMORY VERSE: *"In him was life; and the life was the light of men."* **John 1:4a, GNT**

CENTRAL THOUGHT: *There's a needed separation in order to see things from the Divine perspective.*

Study Headings:

- *Going Forward*
- *Be Humble*
- *Men Like Trees*
- *Separate Yourself*

Study Introduction:

To become the person God wants you to be, you need to move away from people who do not think like God does. As a little boy or girl, there are many people who come your way. Many of them want to be your friends. But not all of them are permitted to be. Only the people who can help you see things from God's standpoint are permitted to be your friend.

Read Mark 8:22-26.

Mark 8:22-26 says, "When they arrived at Bethsaida, some people brought a blind man to Jesus, and they begged him to touch the man and heal him. *Jesus took the blind man by the hand and led him out of the village.* Then, spitting on the man's eyes, he laid his hands on him and asked, "Can you see anything now?" *The man looked around. "Yes," he said, "I see people, but I can't see them very clearly. They look like trees walking around."* Then Jesus placed his hands on the man's eyes again, and his eyes were opened. His sight was completely restored, and he could see everything clearly. Jesus sent him away, saying, "Don't go back into the village on your way home."

This is the familiar story of the blind man in Bethsaida.

When this blind man was brought to Jesus, Jesus took his hand, and basically led Him out of the village. The village here is as simple as his tribe. So, Jesus took him away from the people that he considered to be his tribe, so that He could actually help him see things differently.

Sometimes when you are with the people of your tribe, you begin to see things from a tribal viewpoint. But Jesus wanted this man to take a step forward. He didn't want him to see things from a tribal viewpoint. He wanted him to begin to see from the viewpoint of God.

YOU ARE THAT TREE!

T. S. CHERRY

As a child of God, your Heavenly Father wants you to stop seeing from your viewpoint and that of those around you. God wants to make you into a great man or woman. But He wants you to always ask yourself, "How does God see what I am doing or about to do right now?" That is what this lesson is about.

GOING FORWARD

To move to the next level, God wants you to move away from what is familiar to you and to everyone, to what He wants you to do. Move away from what you always know how to do, to what God wants you to do.

Read Mark 2:12

When Jesus was on earth, He always acted from the viewpoint or perspective of God. He always did what God wanted Him to do. Mark 2:12 says, "They were all completely amazed and praised God, saying, "We have never seen anything like this!"" Why were they amazed? Jesus did what was not familiar to everyone, but what God wanted Him to do.

In the same way, God wants you to move away from what is familiar to you and to everyone, to what He wants you to do.

YOU ARE THAT TREE!

T. S. CHERRY

BE HUMBLE

What was the next thing Jesus did after leading the blind man away from the village? He spat on his eyes and asked him if he could see anything.

This is very humbling. To spit on a person's eyes is basically to lower what that person thinks of himself. As a matter of fact, in the Old Testament, to spit on a person's face was a sign of humiliation.

Read Deuteronomy 25:9.

To accept to be spat on requires real humility.

But, if you really want to change your life, you must be ready to humble yourself to the place where you will accept the truth, even when it feels like it's being 'spit in your eye.' Without this, it'll be difficult to have God

MEN LIKE TREES

As Jesus lays His hands on the blind man, the first thing he sees are men walking around like trees.

Again you see the position meant for you and me. God wants us to be the trees in the midst of the garden. He wants us to be oozing life and blessings to the people around us.

So, God is challenging you to be that tree in the midst of the garden that Daniel is talking about.

Read John 1:4.

YOU ARE THAT TREE! — T. S. CHERRY

NOTE: You are the tree of life because you carry the life of the Savior in you. Jesus in your life makes you bring life to everyone you come in contact with. The Bible says, "In him was life; and the life was the light of men" (John 1:4).

So, you want to move to the next level? You must understand that you are that tree that must bring life to everyone around you.

SEPARATE YOURSELF

What do you ultimately learn from the encounter of the blind man?

You learn that there is a needed separation from the people around you for some time. There's a needed separation in order to see things from God's viewpoint.

1. You need to separate from friends who are not helping you to think like God or see things from His perspective.
2. You need to separate from too much play and begin to read your Bible.
3. You need to separate yourself time after time and talk to God in prayer.

When you do these, you will grow up to be a person who can be sensitive enough to hear the voice of God.

CONCLUSION

To experience the next level in your life, you must move away from some people for a time, just like Jesus took that blind man away from some people. That will help you see things from the viewpoint of God.

REMEMBER THIS:

To see things from God's viewpoint, you must separate yourself.

YOU ARE THAT TREE!

T. S. CHERRY

LESSON 3

TOPIC: TAKE CHARGE OF MY LIFE LORD!

TEXT: Daniel 4:13-14

MEMORY VERSE: *"Then you will admit that the Supreme God controls all human kingdoms and that he can give them to anyone he chooses."* **Daniel 4:25d**

CENTRAL THOUGHT: *God wants to be the center of your life.*

Study Headings:

- *Decide for God*
- *Make God the Center*

Study Introduction:

God has a plan for everyone. This plan is called His pre-ordained plan. That means God had made this plan for your life long before your mother gave birth to you.

Read Jeremiah 29:11. It talks about the fact that God has plans for your life.

Will you like to access the pre-ordained plan of God for your life? Will you like to know what He has made for you to become in life? Then it is time for you to start right now, at this age, to ask the Lord to take charge of your life.

When God takes charge of your life, you won't be that tree full of leaves yet without fruit. No. You will blossom and become a blessing for all to see and benefit. Daddy, mummy, uncles and aunties, and everyone around you will be blessed through you.

DECIDE FOR GOD

Read Daniel 4:13-14.

When Daniel interpreted the king's dream, he revealed that the king was that tree.

But there was something else about the king's dream. In his dream the king saw that someone was told to cut down that tree. If the king was the tree, it means he was going to fall.

Daniel 4:13, 14 says, *"I saw in the visions of my head upon my bed, and, behold, a watcher and an holy one came down from heaven; He cried aloud, and said thus,* **Hew down the tree***, and cut off his branches, shake off his leaves, and scatter his fruit: let the beasts get away from under it, and the fowls from his branches:"*

YOU ARE THAT TREE!

T. S. CHERRY

Why did God ask that the king be brought down and humiliated? Because the king did not make decisions that honored God. He said things that did not bring honor and praise to God.

In your life, you must decide to honor God in what you say and how you live. Do not say things that show that you don't respect God. Do not use words that show that you got everything in your life all by yourself and God didn't help you. It's not right.

When you act as if God does not exist, you may fall out of step with the grace of God. Nebuchadnezzar lost his place because he was out of step with God's grace by means of his decisions and utterances.

Read James 4:6.

The Bible tells us that "God resists the proud, but gives grace to the humble."

You see, a person can be a tree but his decisions can cost him his position.

Think about Adam and Eve who were planted in the Garden of God. But they stopped seeking God and started listening to the serpent. Then they began to operate under a curse.

That was how Nebuchadnezzar lost his position and came under a curse. And the curse was that he would graze with the beast of the field until seven years had passed. Read Daniel 4:24-25.

Whenever you are to make a choice between the tree of life and the tree of knowledge of good and evil, always choose the tree of life, which are the ways of God.

A decision to do the wrong thing will take you further and further away from God, to the place where you lose all of your authority. And that is not what you want.

MAKE GOD THE CENTER

God wants to be the center of your life. He wants to have first place. He wants to be in charge. He wants to be your first priority. God does not want you to make your decisions and then come ask Him to bless them. He wants it the other way around. He wants to make the decisions and you simply follow. If you draw near to God, He will also make you His friend. **Read James 4:8.**

God wants you to bring Him into everything you do as a child. He wants you to talk to Him about everything you need. He wants you to thank Him for everything you receive. So, remember to thank Him when you arrive safely at school and when you get back home. Thank Him for providing you food to eat and good health too.

YOU ARE THAT TREE!

When something bothers you, God wants you to talk to Him first before you talk to anyone else about it. And when everything is working perfectly in your life and that of your loved ones, He wants you to know that He did it. So, you must give Him glory at all times.

King Nebuchadnezzar gave the place or glory that was due God to himself and the result was that God humiliated him. Read Daniel 4:24-25.

God doesn't want you to do this. He wants to be the greatest influence over your life. He wants you to give Him the glory for your life always. Don't praise yourself for what God is doing in your life; praise Him alone!

CONCLUSION

As you grow up, everything in your life will change when you choose to put God in charge and see things from His viewpoint. Learn to prioritize His Word. Let your decisions be based on what He says, not just what you think is right. That is the best recipe for acceleration in life!

REMEMBER THIS:

God wants to be the greatest influence over your life.

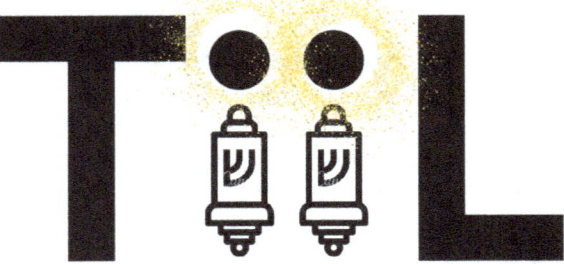

YOU ARE THAT TREE!

T. S. CHERRY

LESSON 4

TOPIC: WATCHING YOUR EVERY STEP

TEXT: Genesis 2:20

MEMORY VERSE: *"But for Adam, no suitable helper was found."* **Genesis 2:20b**

CENTRAL THOUGHT: Godly decisions are more important than good decisions.

Study Headings:

- Barabbas or Jesus?
- A suitable helper
- Your place of authority

Study Introduction:

God does not want you to grow into a stagnant adult, someone whose life isn't going anywhere, and who isn't making any meaningful impact. He wants you to grow into a great person who keeps moving from one position of honor to the next.

So, how do you begin to change your life? It's simple: You stop making good decisions and begin to make godly decisions. To make godly decisions, you need to put God's choices over your own. That is what this lesson is about.

BARABBAS OR JESUS?

Something happened before Jesus was crucified.

The Jews were asked to choose between Jesus and a notorious criminal being freed. They chose Barabbas the notorious criminal instead of Jesus. They rejected the Prince of life.

Read Matthew 27:17,20-21.

As a child of God, every time you are in between making a decision whether to glorify God with your life or not, just remember that you are trying to choose between Barabbas and the King of kings.

Do you know how many times you have asked for Barabbas in your life? Do you know how many people in your life are Barabbas?

Barabbas is the anti-Christ choice. It's the choice that is against God and His will for your life. Always choose Jesus over Barabbas.

Daniel lets us know that people who choose Barabbas over Jesus, are cut down like King Nebuchadnezzar was. God does not allow them stay in their position of authority.

That is not what you want for your life, right? Then you must watch your every step and see that you choose to bring God honor with your choices in life.

A SUITABLE HELPER

God wants you make changes in your life that will bring honor to Him, your King, the One Who died that you may live. One of the areas God wants you to make adequate changes to honor Him and move your life forward, is in the friends you have around you.

You need the right kind of friends – suitable friends around you. **Read Genesis 2:20.**

The Scripture says, *"So the man gave names to all the livestock the birds in the sky, and all the wild beast animals. But for Adam,* **no suitable helper was found.**"

Notice that God didn't say there wasn't a helper found for Adam; He said there wasn't a 'suitable helper.' So, what God wants you to have around you are suitable people – suitable friends.

God wants you to have around you, other children who can help you to be your best for God. If they are not helping you to be a better child of God, you don't have to keep them as your friends.

Use little Samuel as your example. When Eli's children were doing wrong, Samuel refused to join them. He chose the way of God (the tree of life). Read 1Samuel 2:17-18.

Be a Samuel. Align yourself with suitable people. Watch your every step to see that you are guided by God and His Word.

YOU ARE THAT TREE! — T. S. CHERRY

YOUR PLACE OF AUTHORITY

God is raising children who know how to exercise their authority in God. And you must be such a child. To take your place of authority is to know how to make a godly decision. To do that, you must surrender to God totally.

You don't know what's best for your life. God does; He sees everything. To surrender your life to Him is to take your place of authority. That way, you will not be a child with a low self-esteem. You will not exist as a shadow of yourself! You will be confident and perform well in everything.

CONCLUSION

To exercise the authority of God through your life, watch your every step. Watch out for Barabbas and always choose Jesus over him. Make up your mind to surrender fully to God, and He will make you the person He wants you to be.

REMEMBER THIS:

The way to move constantly forward and never backward is to align yourself with suitable people.

YOU ARE THAT TREE!

T. S. CHERRY

LESSON 5

TOPIC: I CHOOSE TO STAND!

TEXT: Genesis 25:22

MEMORY VERSE: *"What is happening now has happened before, and what will happen in the future has happened before,"* **Ecclesiastes 3:15, NLT**

CENTRAL THOUGHT: *Only the Word of God can have absolute impact on the soul.*

Study Headings:

- Body and Soul
- One King
- Let God's Word Rule
- Choose to stand

Study Introduction:

Our study so far shows that every child has the power within them to be the tree of life, which is the expression of God through flesh or to be the tree of good and evil.

In the Scripture, we see Jacob struggle with being the Tree of Life to his people or being a deceiver - a double-minded fellow, that is, the tree of good and evil. This all begins with Jacob's relationship with his brother Esau, and the struggle to express the blessings of God.

How did this all begin? Read about what happened to Rebecca, the mother of Jacob and Esau in **Genesis 25:22-23**.

God told Rebecca that she will give birth to twin boys and the older will be servant to the younger. But it's supposed to be the other way round. That is, the older should lead while the younger follows. But that was not the case with Esau and Jacob. A struggle was the result.

That same struggle is real in our lives, too. Let us see what the struggle is all about, in this lesson.

YOU ARE THAT TREE!

BODY AND SOUL

Before we were created in our body, we first existed in God as a soul. So, when God created us physically, He made a body to house our souls.

That means your soul is pre-existent, and has long existed before your body. Your body only comes into the picture at birth, but the soul has always been.

You see, your soul is older than your body. But now it appears that what God said about Esau and Jacob is playing out between your soul and your body. What that means is that your body always wants to rule over your soul a lot of times.

You will notice this from what happens when you are in between doing something right or wrong. You realize that you are inclined to doing wrong instead of right.

Your body always wants to do the things that will make you feel good, even if God does not like them. But your soul has been with God before you were born, and always wants to please God.

Read 1Peter 2:11.

God uses Peter to tell us that we should run away from those bad things our body wants us to do, because it fights against the soul. And if it fights against the soul, it will eventually destroy our relationship with God.

ONE KING

When we look at the story of Rebecca in the right perspective, we see that, just like Rebecca, there are twins within us jostling for superiority. The soul wants to rule over the body and the body wants to rule over the soul.

But God promised us that the time will come when our body and our soul will both submit to one King - the coming Christ Who would die for our sins.

So, the death of Jesus Christ brought both our body and soul under the rule of ONE KING, which is Jesus Christ or God's Word. **Read Ezekiel 37:22**.

That place says, *"And I will make them* **one nation** *in the land upon the mountains of Israel; and one king shall be king to them all: and they shall be* **no more two nations**, *neither shall they be divided into two kingdoms any more at all:"*

By this prophecy, God wants to bring the conflict of the soul and the body under the Lordship of Jesus Christ. Both of them will be brought under total submission to the Word of God.

LET GOD'S WORD RULE

To be under the rule of ONE KING, you have to allow God's Word rule over your entire life as a young child. That means you will not do anything with your body that God's Word does not permit. You will honor God with every part of your body, including what your eyes see, what your ears hear, and what your mouth speaks.

You must also let the Word of God impact your soul.

Read James 1:21.

That Scripture shows that only the Word of God can have absolute impact on your soul.

Read Hebrews 4:12.

The Apostle Paul writing to the Hebrews about the supremacy of God's Word over both body and soul says, *"For the word of God is alive and powerful. It is sharper than the sharpest two-edged sword,* **cutting between soul and spirit, between joint and marrow.** *It exposes our innermost thoughts and desires"* **(Hebrews 4:12, NLT).**

While "soul and spirit" refer to the pre-existent part of us, "joint and marrow" refer to the body. Paul says that the Word of God bears rule over them all. So, Ezekiel's prophecy comes true: *"and one king shall be king to them all."*

CHOOSE TO STAND

Is there something you are struggling to stop doing? You have to stop struggling and surrender totally to God. Do not allow your body to cause you to do wrong things. Choose to stand up for God by surrendering your body to the Word of God.

Do not allow yourself or anyone else to make you do something that is against the Word of God. Tell yourself, "I choose to stand!"

CONCLUSION

God has brought the conflict of the soul and the body under the Lordship of Jesus Christ. To be under His rule, you have to allow God's Word rule over your entire life as a young child.

REMEMBER THIS:

Only the Word of God can have absolute impact on your life – body and soul.